I'm Pretty Too! Workbook

Step-by-Step Guide to Understanding, Loving and Becoming Your True Self

Created by:
Carrie Jemii

I0192672

ISBN-13: 978-1-945318-07-8
ISBN-10: 1-945318-07-4

To order more Workbooks or request an I'm Pretty Too! Workshop please visit:
www.imprettytoo.org

To Book Me as a Speaker visit:
www.carriejemii.com

Dedication

This workbook is dedicated to every girl and woman who is ready to become unapologetically who they are.

Introduction

Welcome to the I'm Pretty Too! Self-Evaluating Workbook! You are now about to embark on a journey of self-discovery. Exploring areas of Self-Esteem, Self-Image, Self-Worth, Self-Respect and Self-Confidence. If at this point you have been hiding any truths or lies from yourself, they may be revealed. Scared, well don't be this is actually the BEST thing you could ever do for yourself! You are on your way to the best reward life could ever offer you...SELF-LOVE. Well if you're ready...let's get started. At any time, if you do not know the definition of a word research it or ask someone.

Please fill out the following general information about yourself. Try not to think too hard on the answers, go with your first thought. We will use this information later within the book, so be as truthful as possible. If you ever need more space to write please use the "reflection notes" page at the back of each applicable exercise.

Your Name	
Birthday	
Favorite Color	
Favorite Hobby	
A Dream Hobby You Would Like to Start	
Your Favorite Thing About Yourself	
Why?	
Your Least Favorite Thing About Yourself	
Why?	

How would you describe yourself? You can either draw a picture of yourself on the blank page in the back of the book to illustrate this or you can choose to describe yourself in words here.

Read the Lyrics to the song by the artist Mary J. Blige entitled "Take Me as I Am" below and briefly write down what those lyrics mean to you. You can also play the song and listen along as you read the lyrics if you like.

Take Me As I Am –
Mary J. Blige
Song Lyrics

She's been down and out
She's been wrote about
She's been talked about constantly
She's been up and down
She's been pushed around
But they held her down, NYC
She has no regrets
She accepts the past
All these things they
Helped make to make she
She's been lost and found
And she's still around
There's a reason for everything

You know I've been holdin' on
Try to make me weak
But I still stay strong
Put my life all up in these songs
Just so you can feel me
So you can get the real me

So take me as I am
Or have nothing at all (nothing at all)
Just take me as I am
Or have nothing at all (at all)

Now she's older now
Yes, she's wiser now
Can't disguise her now
She don't need
No one tellin' her
What to do and say
No one tellin' her
Who to be
She's on solid ground
She's been lost and found
Now she answers to G-O-D
And she's confident
This is not the end
Ask me how I know
'Cause she is me
You know I've been holdin' on
Try to make me weak

But I still stay strong
Put my life all up in these songs
Just so you can feel me
So you can get the real me

So take me as I am
Or have nothing at all (nothing
at all)
Just take me as I am
Or have nothing at all (at all)

So it's all or nothing at all
All or nothing at all
Don't you know I can only be
me
(I can only be me, yeah)
So it's all or nothing at all
All or nothing at all
Don't you know I can only be
me
(I can only be me, yeah)
So take me as I am
Or have nothing at all (nothing
at all)
Just take me as I am
Or have nothing at all (at all)

This is me!

Day 1
Understanding You: **A Pretty Portrait**

You will start **Day 1** off by pulling back the layers of who you are today, and as we progress through this workbook you will begin to put yourself back together but greater than before! Today and the next few days will explore the areas of Self-Esteem and Self-Image.

Answer the following questions, please allow some reflection time before answering.

Question #1: What are some of the main feelings and emotions you experience every day? (Example: Depression, Unattractiveness, Rejection, Overweight, Too Tall, etc.)

_____

_____

_____

_____

_____

_____

_____

Question #2: Who or what triggers those feelings and emotions?

_____

_____

_____

_____

_____

_____

Question #3: As it relates to question #2, do you have the power in the situation, or does the "what" or "who" has the power? If the answer is not "you" proceed to the next question.

Do you think it is possible for you to regain your power back over those feelings and emotions? Yes, or No. If no, then why not?

On question #3 part 1 & 2, if you answered anything other than You and No, you have to realize that your opinion is the only one that matters. As we progress through this workbook, it is my only hope that this becomes your new reality, it won't be easy but it is possible!

Now that you have recognized your true feelings about yourself, along with the "what" and "who" triggers those feelings, let's figure out how you got here so you can get back to a healthier place with your feelings and emotions towards yourself.

Question #4: Define Self- Image. Use the Merriam-Webster dictionary.

The idea _____ has of _____ Abilities,
A_____, and P_____.

Question #5: Define Self-Esteem. Use Merriam-Webster dictionary.

Confidence in _____ own W_____ or
A _____. Satisfaction in oneself.

After defining Self-Image and Self-Esteem, would you consider your self-image and esteem Positive or Negative?

8

The following chart shows the difference between positive and negative Self-Image/ Self- Esteem.

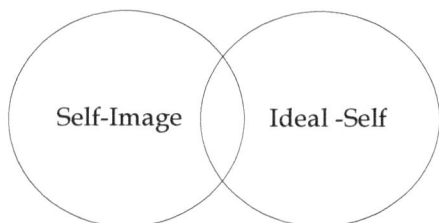

Negative Self Image and Esteem   *Positive Self Image and Esteem*

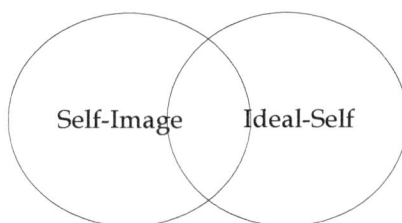

Self-Image   Ideal -Self   Self-Image   Ideal-Self

Unbalanced   *Balanced*

We would all agree that having a positive self-image and esteem is ideal. Based on the illustration above, in order to accomplish a positive outlook, you have to be REAL with yourself. Meaning, ideally ("ideal self"), some of us would love to have a body shape and/or the looks of a model (*based on societal views and opinions of beauty*) however, you were born and formed perfectly the way you are. For that reason alone, you have no cause to apologize for not looking like anyone other than yourself, rather you are short, tall, skinny, thick or have a light or dark complexion. You are unapologetically PRETTY TOO!

That being said, as you take this journey to establish a positive self-image of yourself understand that your ideal self should simply be the best version of you and only you! NO COMPARING. Once you accept that, you will be well on your way to a progressive positive self-image and esteem. Say it LOUD **I'm Pretty Too!**

Day 1 - *Understanding You:* **A Pretty Portrait**

Reflection Notes:

Journal Reflection on Day 1

Reflection Question: reflecting back to page 4 and the question "what is your least favorite thing about you", do you think it's possible to love that "thing" one day and why? Before answering that question find the closet mirror and look at yourself for 60 seconds. Next, answer the above question and then write out some of the steps you can take to love your least favorite thing about yourself?

_____

_____

_____

_____

_____

_____

_____

_____

_____

_____

_____

Enter in Day 2 Affirmation as an alarm for 8:00am in your phone or tablet.

Journal Reflection Day 2

<u>Daily Affirmation</u>: I am who I say I am, and I'm Pretty Too!

(Write a journal entry and have a 7-minute meditation on today's Affirmation)

_____

_____

_____

_____

_____

_____

_____

_____

_____

_____

_____

_____

_____

Journal Reflection Day 3

<u>*Daily Scripture*</u>: "By the grace of God, I am what I am."
I Corinthians 15:10

(Write a journal entry and say a prayer incorporating today's Daily Scripture)

_____

_____

_____

_____

_____

_____

_____

_____

_____

_____

_____

_____

_____

_____

Journal Reflection Day 4

Daily Question: What Makes "Me" Happy?

(Write a journal entry answering the above question)

_____

_____

_____

_____

_____

_____

_____

_____

_____

_____

_____

_____

_____

_____

_____

Enter in Day 5 Affirmation as an alarm for 8:00am in your phone or tablet.

Journal Reflection Day 5

Daily Affirmation: I am AMAZING regardless of what anyone thinks, I'm Pretty Too!

(Write a journal entry and have a 7-minute meditation on today's Affirmation)

_____

_____

_____

_____

_____

_____

_____

_____

_____

_____

_____

_____

_____

_____

_____

_____

Journal Reflection Day 6

Daily Scripture: "You are beautiful for you are fearfully and wonderfully made." Psalms 139:14

(Write a journal entry and say a prayer incorporating today's Daily Scripture)

Journal Reflection Day 7

Daily Question: I am GRATEFUL for?

(Write a journal entry answering the above question)

Day 8
Understanding You: **A Pretty Portrait**

You will start **Day 8** by briefly reflecting on the last 7 days of journal entries. After reflecting, take 7-minutes to mediate. Mediate on clearing out all of the negative voices and opinions in your head, that are opposing to what you feel about yourself. Afterwards, answer the questions below, remember to allow some reflection time before answering.

Question #1: Describe how you feel about yourself today?

_____

_____

_____

_____

_____

_____

_____

_____

_____

Question #2: Go to the closest mirror and write down (5) pretty things about you.

1. _____

_____

2 _____

_____

3. _____

_____

4 _____

_____

5 _____

_____

Day 8 - *Understanding You:* **A Pretty Portrait**

Reflection Notes:

Now, let's have a little fun!

Reflection Activity. You can either do activity (1) or (2), or both.

Activity (1) Create a Newsletter, that's all about you! In this newsletter, you will write a few articles that are just about you…an "About Me" article, that has some interesting facts that people didn't know about you, the "Things I Like About Myself" article, where I want you to focus on all the great things about you and last but not least the <u>must have</u> article called "Why I Don't Care What You Think?". In this article section, I want you to capture all your thoughts and feelings on why you will no longer care about what people think about you!

(A Special Note: Just to clarify: *There is a HUGE difference between people's negative opinions or thoughts about you that are intended to hurt you (destructive criticism) vs. someone trying to assist you in being a better version of yourself (constructive criticism). Constructive criticism can seem or even feel negative and somewhat uncomfortable; however, it is usually intended to help you be better in some weak areas in either your life, personality, schoolwork or career.*)

Activity (2) Draw a stick figure of yourself and label the parts of the body, the Head, Mouth, Ears, Right Arm, Left Arm, Heart, Left Leg and Right Leg. For each part of the body give it a positive attribute for instance **Ears** – "to only hear things that uplift me or make me a better person" ('constructive criticism'). **Right Arm –** "to embrace those who show love to me, etc.". Have fun with this activity and remember it's all about you beautiful! The point of these activities is for you to love who you are.

On the following two pages, I have provided you templates to use for both activities if you like, or you can create your own.

The DAILY NEWS

About Me:

[Place Image Here]

Things I Like About Myself:

Why I Don't Care What You Think:

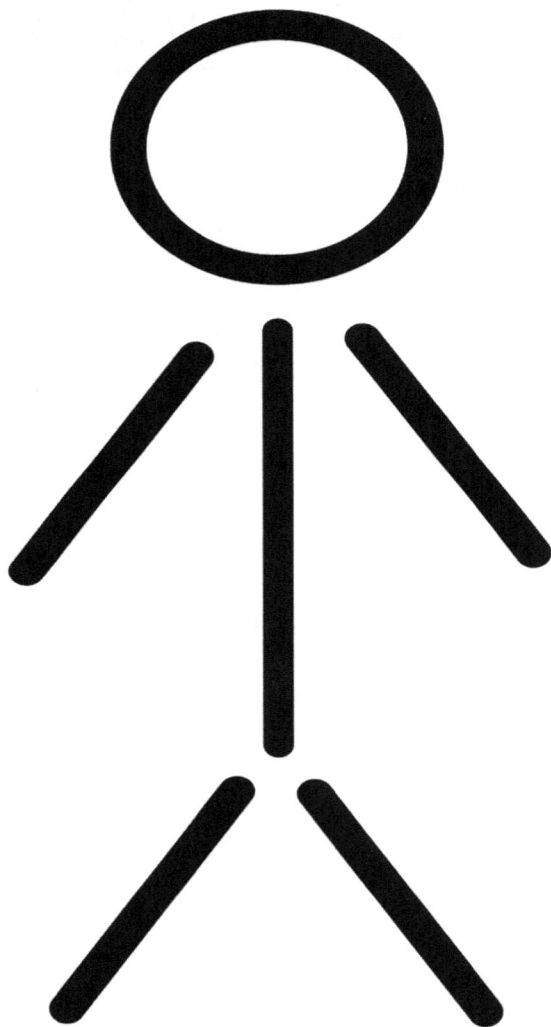

Journal Reflection on Day 8

Reflection Question: on Day 8, how would you describe your self-image and self-esteem? Be honest. If there is no change it is okay, remember this is a journey, things won't happen overnight but they should become better day by day. Be patient with yourself, you have time!

(Write a journal entry answering the above question)

_____

_____

_____

_____

_____

_____

_____

_____

_____

_____

_____

_____

_____

_____

_____

Enter in Day 9 Affirmation as an alarm for 8:00am in your phone or tablet.

Journal Reflection Day 9

Daily Affirmation: I Love Who I Am Becoming.

(Write a journal entry and have a 7-minute meditation on today's Affirmation)

_____

_____

_____

_____

_____

_____

_____

_____

_____

_____

_____

_____

_____

_____

Journal Reflection Day 10

Daily Scripture: "I loved you at your darkest." Romans 5:8

(Write a journal entry and say a prayer incorporating today's Daily Scripture)

Journal Reflection Day 11

Daily Question: What are some negative contributing factors to my low self-esteem? How can I prevent them from affecting me in the future?

(Write a journal entry answering the above question)

_____

_____

_____

_____

_____

_____

_____

_____

_____

_____

_____

_____

_____

_____

_____

Enter in Day 12 Affirmation as an alarm for 8:00am in your phone or tablet.

Journal Reflection Day 12

<u>*Daily Affirmation:*</u> The Best Thing I Can Do Is Believe ME!

(Write a journal entry and have a 7-minute meditation on today's Affirmation)

_____

_____

_____

_____

_____

_____

_____

_____

_____

_____

_____

_____

_____

_____

_____

_____

_____

Journal Reflection Day 13

<u>*Daily Scripture*</u>: "I am complete in Him." Colossians 2:10

(Write a journal entry and say a prayer incorporating today's Daily Scripture)

Journal Reflection Day 14

Daily Question: After two weeks writing in this journey...I feel?

(Write a journal entry answering the above question)

_____

_____

_____

_____

_____

_____

_____

_____

_____

_____

_____

_____

_____

_____

_____

_____

_____

_____

Day 15
Loving You: **Pretty Worth It!**

We will start **Day15** diving right into the areas of Self-Worth and Self-Respect. Answer the questions below, and remember to allow some reflection time before answering.

Question #1: Define Self-Worth. Use Dictionary.com.

The sense of _____ own V_____ or
_____ as a person.

Question #2: Define Self-Respect. Use Google the search engine.

P_____ and _____ in oneself. A feeling that one is behaving with H_____ and D _____.

Question #3: How would you rate your self-worth? How do you value yourself? (*For example, high, in the middle or low.*)

_____

_____

_____

_____

_____

Question #4 Has anyone ever tried to diminish your worth or even determine your worth for you?

_____

_____

_____

_____

Question #5: Write down one word that you want people to see when they look at you?

Describe what that looks like? Is that how you present yourself today?

Day 15 - *Loving You: **Pretty Worth It!***

Reflection Notes:

Journal Reflection on Day 15

Reflection Question, today is still day 15 and I want you to reflect on how you present yourself. Presentation is everything. How you present yourself determines how people will respect you. What does your presentation say about you, e.g. how you dress, how you talk, how you respect others...etc.?

(Write a journal entry answering the above question)

_____

_____

_____

_____

_____

_____

_____

_____

_____

_____

_____

_____

_____

_____

Enter in Day 16 Affirmation as an alarm for 8:00am in your phone or tablet.

Journal Reflection Day 16

Daily Affirmation: I am Worth It *because* I deserve to feel PRETTY.

(Write a journal entry and have a 7-minute meditation on today's Affirmation)

_____

_____

_____

_____

_____

_____

_____

_____

_____

_____

_____

_____

_____

_____

_____

_____

Journal Reflection Day 17

Daily Scripture: Who can find a virtuous woman? for her worth *is* far above rubies. Proverbs 31:10

(Write a journal entry and say a prayer incorporating today's Daily Scripture)

Journal Reflection Day 18

Daily Question: The respect you have for yourself determines your worth. Knowing this, how will you start presenting yourself to the world in the future?

(Write a journal entry answering the above question)

_____

_____

_____

_____

_____

_____

_____

_____

_____

_____

_____

_____

_____

_____

_____

Enter in Day 19 Affirmation as an alarm for 8:00am in your phone or tablet.

Journal Reflection Day 19

Daily Affirmation: I respect myself too much to settle for less than I deserve.

(Write a journal entry and have a 7-minute meditation on today's Affirmation)

Journal Reflection Day 20

Daily Scripture: "Whenever you feel unloved, unimportant, or insecure, remember to whom you belong." Ephesians 2:19-22

(Write a journal entry and say a prayer incorporating today's Daily Scripture)

Journal Reflection Day 21

Daily Question: Who Am I?

(Write a journal entry answering the above question)

_____

_____

_____

_____

_____

_____

_____

_____

_____

_____

_____

_____

_____

_____

_____

_____

Day 22
Loving You: **Pretty Worth It!**

Day 22 Every day we are in a silent auction, people bidding on your beauty, your worth, your talents and how much or little to respect you. In being "woke" to this understanding, answer the following questions below, remember to allow some reflection time before answering.

Question #1: How would you rate your self-worth today (*high, in the middle or low*)? How do you value yourself today? Has it changed in last 7 days and why?

_____

_____

_____

_____

_____

_____

_____

_____

_____

_____

We place value on things around us all the time. So, when someone see you, you want their first thought to be "she is priceless, indispensable" ... because you are! If they don't recognize that, they are not worth your time!

Reflection Activity. As you fill out the chart on the next page, you will realize the worth and value we place on certain items. The good thing is that you too determine your own value. As you see the retail value (*"what consumers pay"*) is actually worth way more than the production cost of the item. That is because you *("the consumer")* have placed that value on that item. The same way people will place value on you if you don't set your own WORTH and make it non-negotiable! *You will need the internet to complete this activity.*

Item name	Retail Price (Value)	Production Cost
Nike Gym Shoes	$100+	$12 or less (true!)
Cell Phone		
Hair Extensions		
Name Brand Jeans		
You		

Day 22 – *Loving You: **Pretty Worth It!***

Reflection Notes:

Journal Reflection on Day 22

<u>*Reflection Question*</u>: how important is your Self-Worth and
Self- Respect to you?

(Write a journal entry answering the above question)

_____

_____

_____

_____

_____

_____

_____

_____

_____

_____

_____

_____

_____

_____

Enter in Day 23 Affirmation as an alarm for 8:00am in your phone or tablet.

Journal Reflection Day 23

<u>*Daily Affirmation*</u>: I am Worth It *because* I say I am Worth it!

(Write a journal entry and have a 7-minute meditation on today's Affirmation)

_____

_____

_____

_____

_____

_____

_____

_____

_____

_____

_____

_____

_____

Journal Reflection Day 24

Daily Scripture: "Charm is deceptive and beauty is fleeting, but a woman who fears the Lord is to be praised." Proverbs 31:30

(Write a journal entry and say a prayer incorporating today's Daily Scripture)

Daily Question: Other than valuing Yourself what are some other things you value in life, e.g. Family, Close Friends, Health and Integrity… and why?

(Write a journal entry answering the above question)

_____

_____

_____

_____

_____

_____

_____

_____

_____

_____

_____

_____

_____

_____

_____

Enter in Day 26 Affirmation as an alarm for 8:00am in your phone or tablet.

Journal Reflection Day 26

Daily Affirmation: I will never allow anyone to disrespect me.

(Write a journal entry and have a 7-minute meditation on today's Affirmation)

_____

_____

_____

_____

_____

_____

_____

_____

_____

_____

_____

_____

_____

_____

_____

_____

Daily Scripture: "It is not fancy hair, gold jewelry, or fine clothes that should make you beautiful. No, your beauty should come from inside you –the beauty of a gentle and quiet spirit. That beauty will never disappear and it is worth very much to God." 1 Peter 3:3-4

(Write a journal entry and say a prayer incorporating today's Daily Scripture)

Journal Reflection Day 28

<u>*Daily Question*</u>: What are 10 things that you are thankful for?
Reflect on these things today.

(Write a journal entry answering the above question)

Day 29
Becoming You: **A Pretty Conqueror!**

It is **Day 29** and you are almost 30 days into rediscovering who you really are! Not what someone told you that you were, but who you know yourself to be! Feels great, right?! You understand, you've learn to love, now you BECOME! Become the new and improved you with complete confidence, building yourself one step, one day at a time. Answer the following questions below, remember to allow some reflection time before answering.

Question #1: Fill in the charts below.

List 5 of your Strengths	List 5 of your Weakness/Challenges
1.	1.
2.	2.
3.	3.
4.	4.
5.	5.

Think of one good way to improve your weakness/challenge above.

Weakness/Challenge	Way to Improve
1.	1.
2.	2.
3.	3.
4.	4.
5.	5.

Question #2: Define Confidence. Use Merriam-Webster dictionary.

A feeling of S_____ arising from _____ appreciation of _____ own A_____ or Q_____.

Question #3: List (3) of your most recent Accomplishments.

1. _____

_____

2. _____

_____

3 _____

_____

Question #4: Fill in the chart below.

List 5 Goals you want to Accomplish	Target Completion Date
1.	
2.	
3.	
4.	
5.	

Accomplishing the goals you set for yourself is a clear way to improve your self-confidence.

Try it!

Question #5: Complete this exercise. Be honest with yourself. After completion read aloud the positive thoughts in the mirror on a daily basis. Once this becomes routine, the thoughts will become your reality.

Negative Limiting Thought	Positive Enabling Thought
I'm a loser nothing ever works for me	I AM a winner! I have succeeded with many things.
I'm unlikable, nobody like me	I AM loved by many people
I am unattractive	I AM Pretty Too!
I'm not smart, it takes me a long time to learn things.	I AM intelligent! I persevere until I learn.

When reading add **"I'm Pretty Too!"** to the end of each
Positive Enabling Thought Statement

Ultimately, what you think you will become. In order to become a better version of yourself you have to change the way you think about yourself. The activity above is one step in helping you to achieve that. It also allows you to focus on your strengths vs. negative things that limit your potential. You should feel great about yourself. But we will not stop here, we will continue to grow and continue to build your confidence by taking on new goals and accomplishing them too.

If you say can't then you won't. From this day forward you have to take control of your thoughts and how you perceive yourself. You are a game changer! The world is waiting on you…on your strengths, your unique talents, things that <u>only</u> you can do! It's time to make all your dreams come true, and fulfill whatever desires you have in your heart! You can and you will do it! It's Your Time! Shine bright beautiful! Shine bright!

Day 29 - *Becoming You:* ***A Pretty Conqueror!***

Reflection Notes:

Journal Reflection on Day 29

Reflection Question: now that you know how great you are, how do you plan on making your mark on the world?

(Write a journal entry answering the above question)

_____

_____

_____

_____

_____

_____

_____

_____

_____

_____

_____

_____

_____

_____

_____

Enter in Day 30 Affirmation as an alarm for 8:00am in your phone or tablet.

Journal Reflection Day 30

Daily Affirmation: I AM GOOD ENOUGH.

(Write a journal entry and have a 7-minute meditation on today's Affirmation)

_____

_____

_____

_____

_____

_____

_____

_____

_____

_____

_____

_____

_____

_____

_____

_____

_____

Journal Reflection Day 31

Daily Scripture: "God is within her, she will not fall." Psalm 46:5

(Write a journal entry and say a prayer incorporating today's Daily Scripture)

Journal Reflection Day 32

Daily Question: What are some things that you can do to continue to build your self-confidence?

(Write a journal entry answering the above question)

_____

_____

_____

_____

_____

_____

_____

_____

_____

_____

_____

_____

_____

_____

_____

Enter in Day 33 Affirmation as an alarm for 8:00am in your phone or tablet.

Journal Reflection Day 33

Daily Affirmation: I make a difference.

(Write a journal entry and have a 7-minute meditation on today's Affirmation)

_____

_____

_____

_____

_____

_____

_____

_____

_____

_____

_____

_____

_____

_____

Journal Reflection Day 34

Daily Scripture: "She is clothed with strength and dignity, and she laughs without fear of the future." Proverbs 31:25

(Write a journal entry and say a prayer incorporating today's Daily Scripture)

Journal Reflection Day 35

Daily Question: Reflecting back on day 1, how would you feel about starting that dream hobby tomorrow?

(Write a journal entry answering the above question)

_____

_____

_____

_____

_____

_____

_____

_____

_____

_____

_____

_____

_____

_____

_____

_____

_____

Day 36
Becoming You: **A Pretty Conqueror!**

It is **Day 36,** have you thought about what is next for you? How you see yourself in the future? What would you like to see in the future? These are questions that you may be asking yourself. Well this next reflection activity will help you to not only think about it but actually visualize it!

Our last reflection activity is creating a Vision Board! It's my favorite activity to do every year and after one has been fully achieved.

Reflection Activity. To create the ultimate vision board, you will a medium to large white board, old and/or new magazines, newspapers, markers, glue stick and/or invisible tape, scissors and markers.

Now what you want to do is to cut all pictures and words that apply to what you want in the future out. Rather that is a new body (becoming healthier), better grades, high school/college choices, career change...whatever you want! Find it, cut it out and paste/tape it to your white board. This can be as messy or as organized as you want, it's your board. Afterwards, find some place special in your house where you can put the vision board and look at it from time to time or everyday if you like.

Having this visual aid will assist you in accomplishing your goals and making your dreams come true. Like I stated before, what you think is what you ultimately will become. So, if you think you will be wealthy, you will become wealthy. If you think you have high self-esteem, self-worth and self-confidence, you will have it!

Enjoy the last 14 days of this journey! It's almost over! Finish strong and be proud of the girl/woman you are BECOMING!

Enter in Day 37 Affirmation as an alarm for 8:00am in your phone or tablet.

Journal Reflection Day 37

Daily Affirmation: I AM Confident!

(Write a journal entry and have a 7-minute meditation on today's Affirmation)

_____

_____

_____

_____

_____

_____

_____

_____

_____

_____

_____

_____

_____

_____

_____

Journal Reflection Day 38

Daily Scripture: "Don't worry about anything, instead, pray about everything. Tell God what you need, and thank Him for all He has done." Philippians 4:6-8

(Write a journal entry and say a prayer incorporating today's Daily Scripture)

_____

_____

_____

_____

_____

_____

_____

_____

_____

_____

_____

_____

_____

_____

_____

Daily Question: If you could write a brief letter to that "who" or "what" that ever made you feel differently than how you feel about yourself today, what would you say?

(Write a journal entry answering the above question)

_____

_____

_____

_____

_____

_____

_____

_____

_____

_____

_____

_____

_____

_____

Enter in Day 40 Affirmation as an alarm for 8:00am in your phone or tablet.

Journal Reflection Day 40

Daily Affirmation: I can do all things!

(Write a journal entry and have a 7-minute meditation on today's Affirmation)

_____

_____

_____

_____

_____

_____

_____

_____

_____

_____

_____

_____

_____

_____

_____

Journal Reflection Day 41

Daily Scripture: "For I know the plans I have for you."
Jeremiah 29:11

(Write a journal entry and say a prayer incorporating today's Daily Scripture)

_____

_____

_____

_____

_____

_____

_____

_____

_____

_____

_____

_____

_____

_____

_____

_____

_____

Journal Reflection Day 42

Daily Question: Are you becoming who you want to be? And if so, how do you plan on keeping her around?

(Write a journal entry answering the above question)

_____

_____

_____

_____

_____

_____

_____

_____

_____

_____

_____

_____

_____

_____

_____

_____

Day 43

Understanding, Loving and Becoming You: **Look How Far You've Come**

Welcome to **Day 43,** and we going to reflect on all three modules now, (1) Self-Esteem/Self-Image, (2) Self-Worth/Self-Respect and (3) Self-Confidence. Answer the following questions below, remember to allow some reflection time before answering.

Question #1: What is your favorite thing or things about you? Why?

_____

_____

_____

_____

Question #2: What is your least favorite thing about you? Why?

_____

_____

Question #3: Which image below best describes you today and why?

Negative Self Image and Esteem   *Positive Self Image and Esteem*

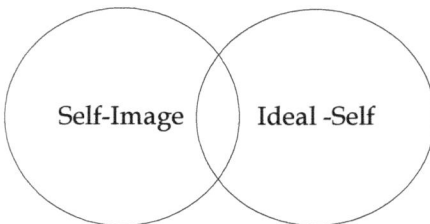

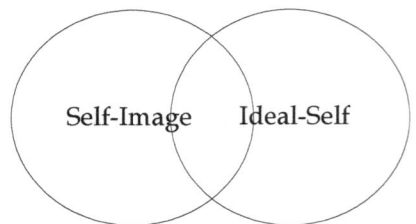

Unbalanced   *Balanced*

_____

_____

_____

_____

_____

_____

Question #4: How would you describe how you feel about yourself today? Any Triggers?

_____

_____

_____

_____

_____

Question #5: How would you rate your self-worth today?

_____

_____

_____

_____

Question #6: Did you improve in any of your weaknesses/challenges, if so which ones and how?

_____

_____

_____

_____

_____

Question #7: On a scale of 1-10, how much has your outlook on yourself changed. Why?

_____

_____

_____

_____

_____

Day 43

Understanding, Loving and Becoming You: **Look How Far You've Come**

Reflection Notes:

The SPECIAL 7

These last seven days are special, and we are going to figure out the most important questions about yourself...why do you love you! Take your time and try not to skip ahead! Answers can be short and quick or long and detailed, but as always, remember to allow some reflection time before answering.

Day 1

I love myself because?

_____

_____

_____

_____

_____

_____

_____

_____

_____

_____

_____

_____

_____

_____

_____

_____

SPECIAL 7

Day 2

Why do you love that about you?
(Referring back to the Special 7 Day 1 entry)

_____

_____

_____

_____

_____

_____

_____

_____

_____

_____

_____

_____

_____

_____

_____

_____

SPECIAL 7

Day 3

And, Why is that?
(Referring back to the Special 7 Day 2 entry)

SPECIAL 7

Day 4

And why is that? (This is a real exercise I learned...)
(Referring back to the Special 7 Day 3 entry)

SPECIAL 7

Day 5

Because why? (Come on don't stop...)
(Referring back to the Special 7 Day 4 entry)

SPECIAL 7

Day 6

And why is that? (I am laughing with you, I promise it has purpose.)
(Referring back to the Special 7 Day 5 entry)

SPECIAL 7

Day 7

And why?
(Referring back to the Special 7 Day 6 entry)

_____

_____

_____

_____

_____

_____

_____

_____

_____

_____

_____

_____

_____

_____

_____

_____

That last statement that you're about to write or already wrote is the real reason why you love yourself! Now don't you ever forget this WHY! When things get challenging again and believe me they will, come back and read this statement.

Cheers to loving the most important person in the world...YOU! Congratulations on finishing this workbook. At any time feel free to answer questions, recite affirmations or read scriptures as much as needed. This is your start to a new and greater you.

I'm Pretty Too! Pledge

Now that you have finished this workbook and/or workshop, I need for you to take a very important pledge, it reads as follows:

I _____ pledge to love myself and to

never return to the girl/woman I was 7 weeks ago. I pledge to

continue to build my self-esteem and self-image. I pledge to know my

worth as a girl/woman and how valuable I am. I pledge to respect

myself and others at all times. I pledge to become the most confident

girl/woman I know. I am that girl! I am beautiful, I am smart, I am

unique, I am unapologetically who I am…

I AM PRETTY TOO!

_____   _____

      Your Signature   Completion Date

_____

      Witness

www.ingramcontent.com/pod-product-compliance
Lightning Source LLC
Chambersburg PA
CBHW070011100426

42741CB00012B/3195